Yesterday

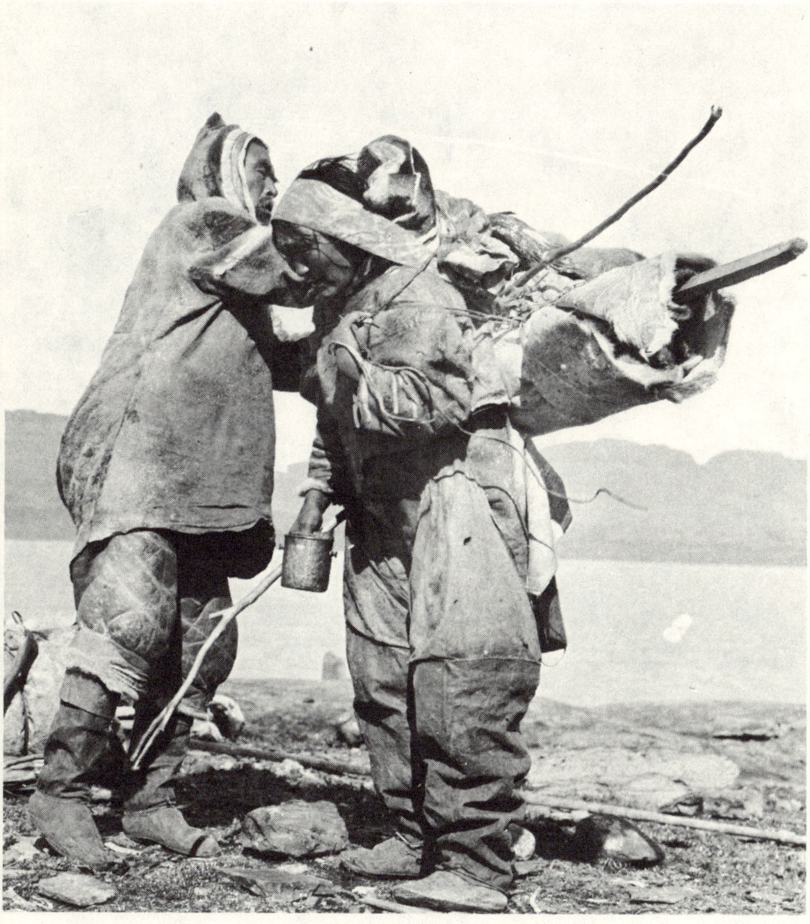

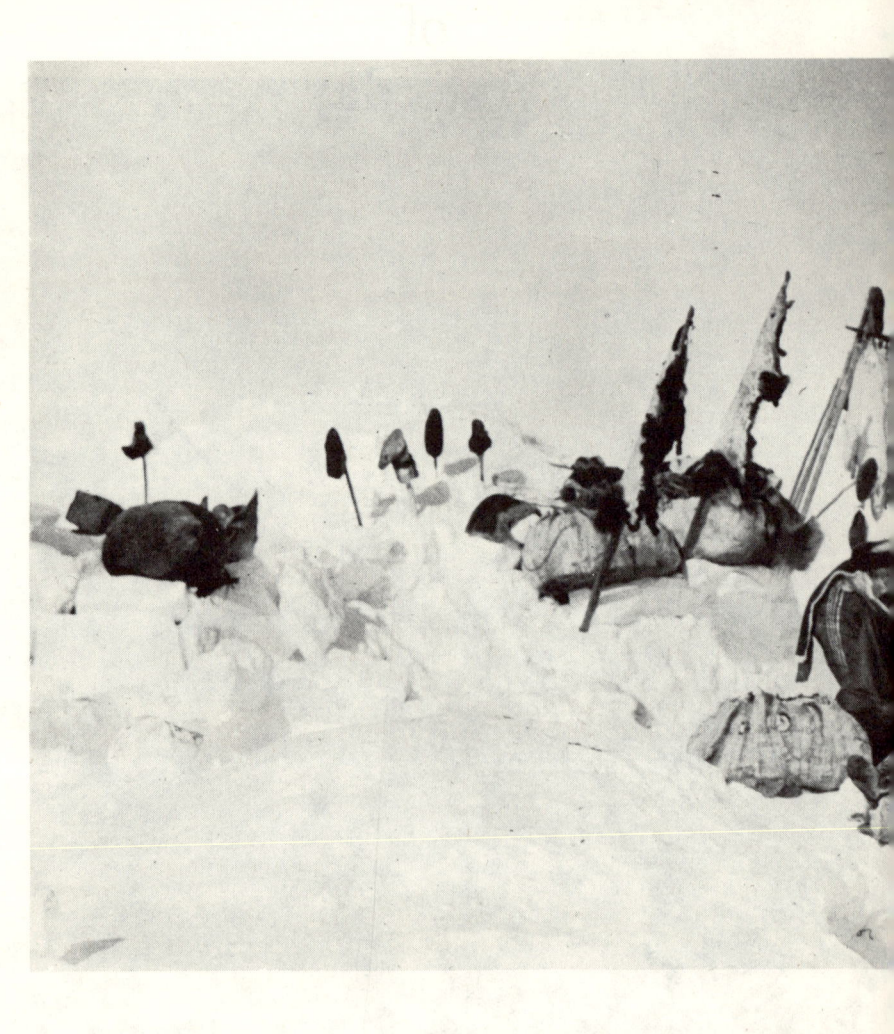

ESKIMO LIFE OF YESTERDAY

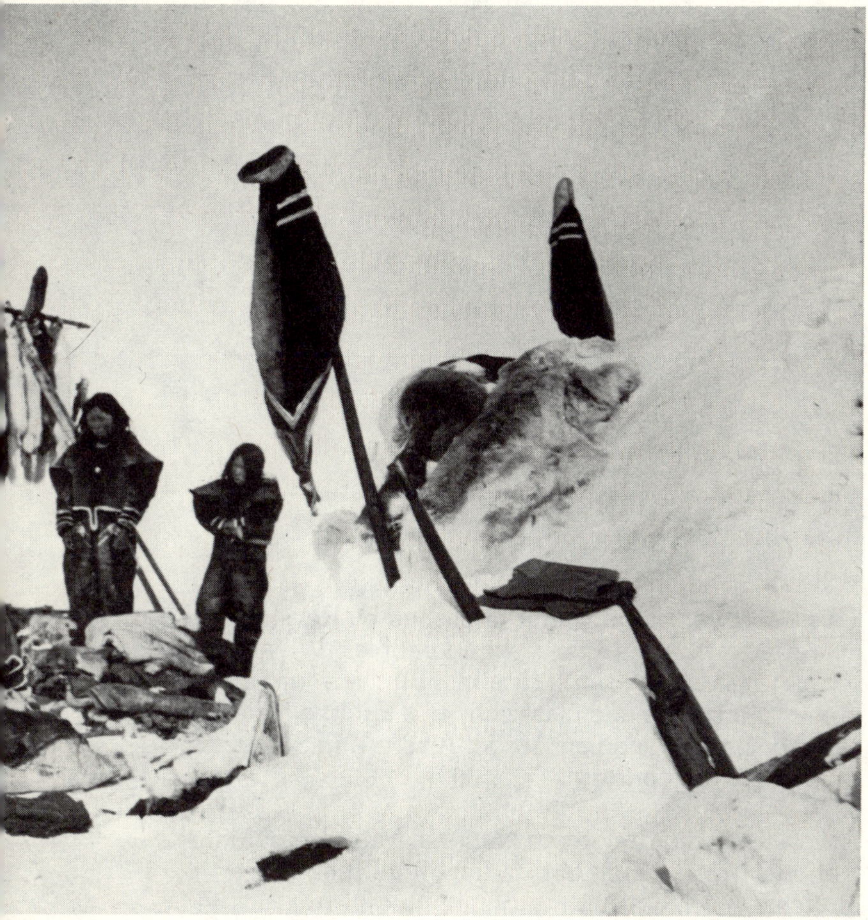

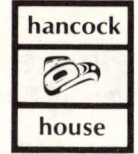

ISBN 0-919654-73-8
Copyright © 1983 Hancock House

Printed in Canada

Catalog in Publication Data

Main entry under title:

Eskimo life of yesterday

ISBN 0-919654-73-8

1. Eskimos - Pictorial works.
E99.E7E85   970'.004'97   C77-00200660-7

All rights reserved. No part of this publication may be reproduced, stored in a retrieval system, or transmitted, in any form or by any means, electronic, mechanical, photocopying, recording or otherwise, without the prior written permission of Hancock House Publishers.

This book was, in part, first published by Revillon Frères as a tribute to the Eskimo peoples. We are reprinting it for the same reasons. Furthermore it presents a simple and classic view of Eskimo life from Labrador, the Canadian Arctic, Alaska and Siberia at the turn of the century.

Special thanks are due the National Museum of Man, National Museum of Canada for use of their fine photos.
PUBLISHED SIMULTANEOUSLY
IN CANADA AND UNITED STATES BY:

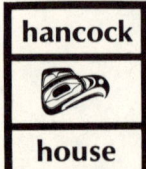

Hancock House Publishers Ltd.
19313 Zero Avenue, Surrey, B.C. V3S 5J9

Hancock House Publishers Inc.
1431 Harrison Avenue, Blaine, Washington, U.S.A. 98230

Contents

- 7 THE ESKIMO FAMILY AT HOME
- 15 A LIVELIHOOD IN THE ARCTIC
- 22 THE EFFICIENT ESKIMO WOMAN
- 29 FRIEND AND SERVANT
  —THE HUSKY DOG
- 37 HAPPY LITTLE ESKIMOS
- 41 KYAK AND OMIAK
- 45 FUR TRADING IN THE NORTH

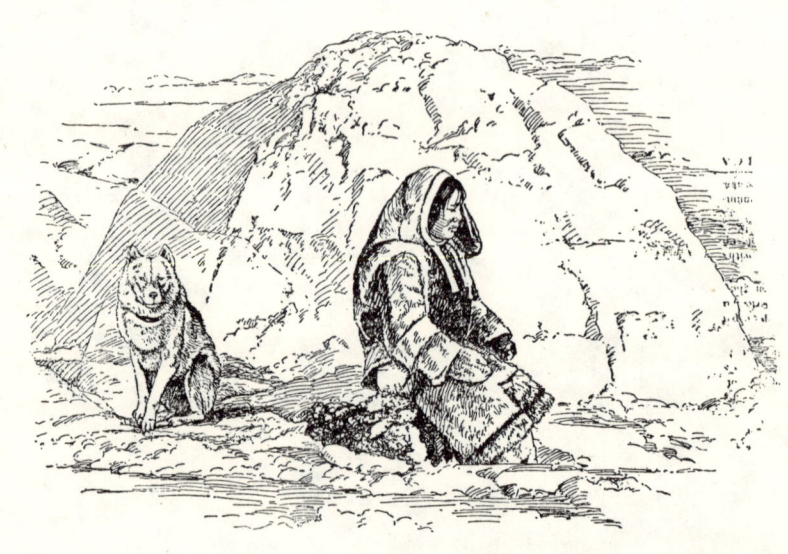

ENJOYING THE ARCTIC SUNSHINE. TO PREVENT FROST-BITE THIS ESKIMO WOMAN DIGS A HOLE IN THE SNOW FOR HER FEET

ESKIMO LIFE

THE ESKIMO FAMILY AT HOME

Leagues and leagues beyond the last tree large enough to afford building material, where icy Arctic gales sweep over the frozen earth for three fourths of the year, the Eskimo preserves his primitive civilization from generation to generation largely through his skill in building his snow house, the igloo.

Every Eskimo family has a summer home and a winter home. Neither of these can be permanent as the scarcity of food in the North means constant and laborious migrations. In summer a tent of skins, which can be carried from place to place, affords shelter enough but when the freezing weather comes—and it comes early in the North—the Eskimo must have a dwelling which can not be blown over or penetrated by searching wind. It must be built quickly in some place where there is a likelihood of obtaining food, so the Eskimo father takes his snow knife and starts an igloo.

His skill at this work is amazing. A row of snow blocks is set in a true circle and other rows are added until there is a beehive-shaped structure on the architectural lines of a dome. The snow blocks

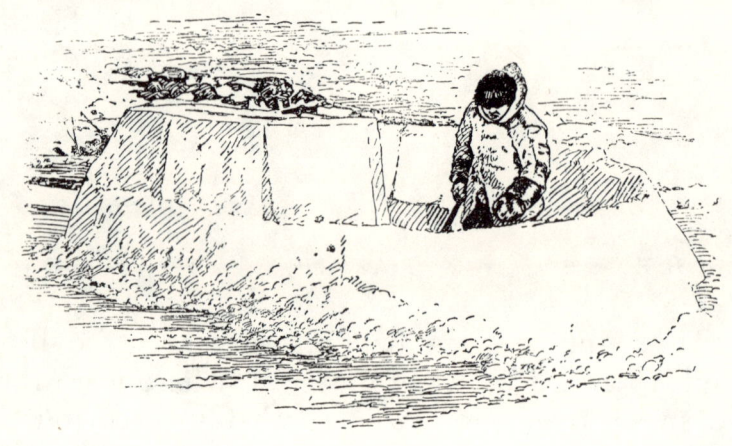

ESKIMO BUILDER
STARTING AN IGLOO

which are soft when cut, freeze together until in a few hours the igloo roof will bear the weight of several persons. About the only thing which will crush it in is a wandering polar bear. An old man and old woman living near the Revillon Post at Cape Dufferin were awakened one night by a polar bear which had broken their roof and thrust his head through the hole only a few feet from their faces. The old woman took the dip used to trim her lamp and held the bear at bay until the old man had hobbled out, secured his harpoon and killed the bear outside the igloo.

The only heat in an igloo is from the lamp which burns seal oil or whale oil with a wick of dried moss. This lamp smokes villainously unless it is tended with great skill. No one ever learns how to manage the native lamp except the Eskimo woman. Care must be taken that the igloo does not get too warm or the walls will begin to drip. The art is to keep the temperature barely below the freezing point. If the Eskimo wife finds her walls getting damp and cannot control the heat otherwise, she pokes a hole in the side of the igloo. When it has cooled sufficiently the hole is mended with soft snow which quickly freezes fast to the original wall. It is important to keep the inside of the igloo dry, not only for the comfort of the occupants but to prevent the fur clothing of the family getting wet. Drying it in the short sunless winter days is almost impossible.

If an Eskimo can get a few tent poles from the trader he builds a drying rack outside his igloo, where clothing may be dried out of reach of the

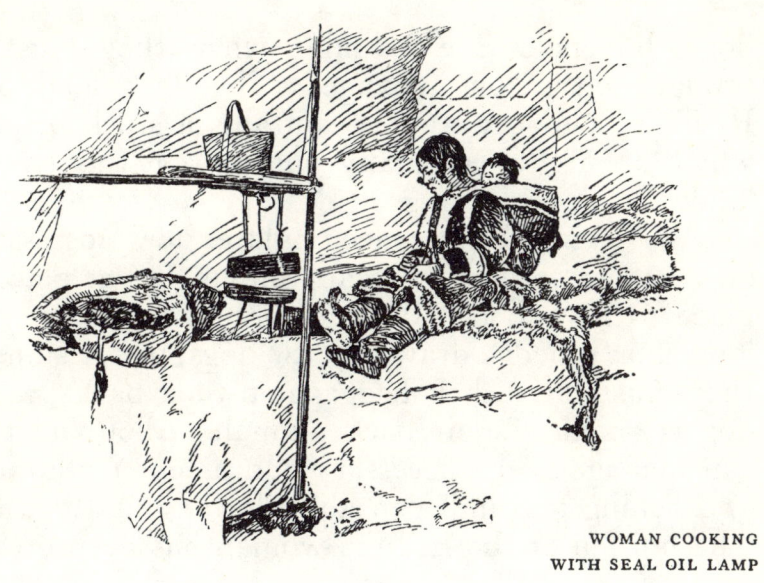

WOMAN COOKING WITH SEAL OIL LAMP

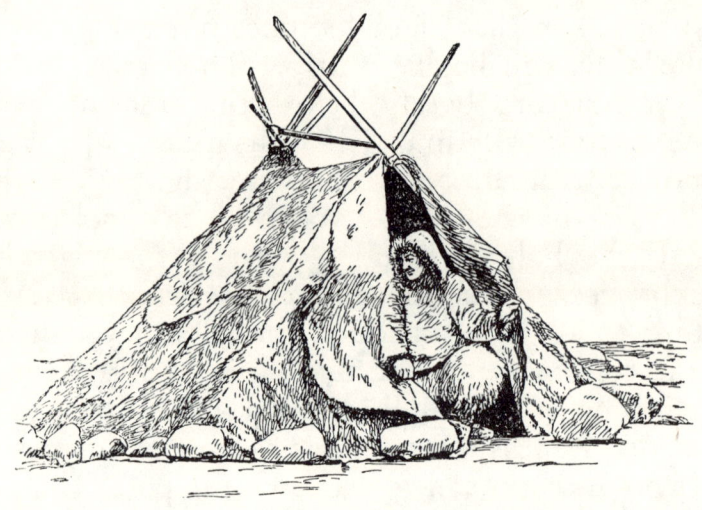

SUMMER TENT OF CARIBOU SKINS ON FISHING SPEARS. IT IS HELD IN PLACE WITH LARGE STONES

dogs, but poles are valuable when they must be brought on a long voyage. The deck load of a Revillon schooner usually contains a stack of poles which are useful for many purposes in this treeless land.

An Eskimo family accumulates few possessions on account of their constant moving from place to place to find food. In winter their goods may be loaded on a sledge drawn by the dogs, but in summer they must carry their baggage on their backs, as the dog is an indifferent pack animal. About all they can manage is the necessary equipment for hunting and fishing and indispensable clothing and utensils. The burden of the Eskimo woman has been greatly lightened by the post trader who has brought within her reach light, strong cooking utensils which she can carry from place to place. These are much better than her home-made containers of walrus hide or the massive stone pots hewn out by her husband with a bow drill.

Igloo life in winter is enlivened by the presence of a litter or two of the carefully bred Malamute puppies which are the Eskimo's most valuable possession. While young they are gentle and lovable and make excellent playmates for the Eskimo children. After his first winter the husky dog must live outdoors, as when grown he is perpetually hungry and will not only eat up the family store of provisions but the deerhide clothing and the sealskin boots.

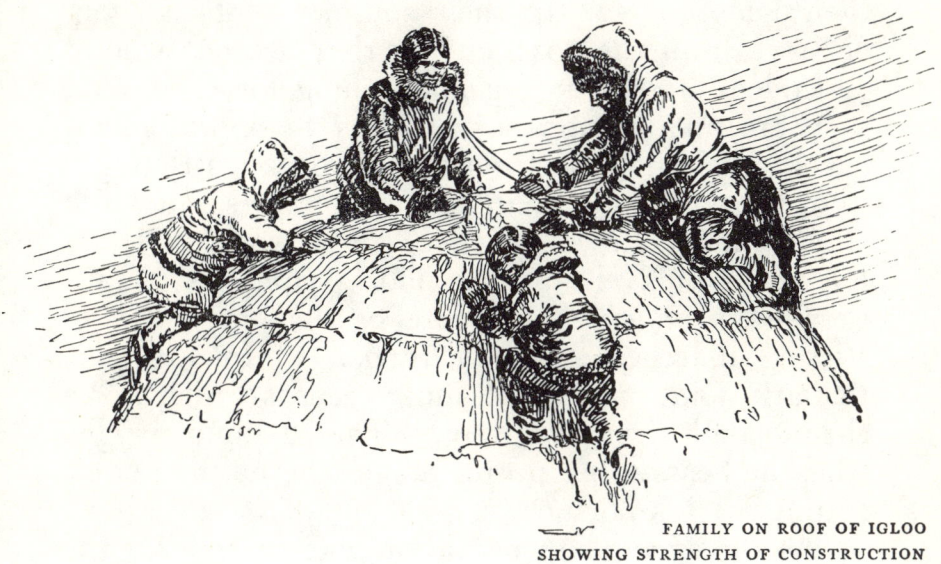

FAMILY ON ROOF OF IGLOO
SHOWING STRENGTH OF CONSTRUCTION

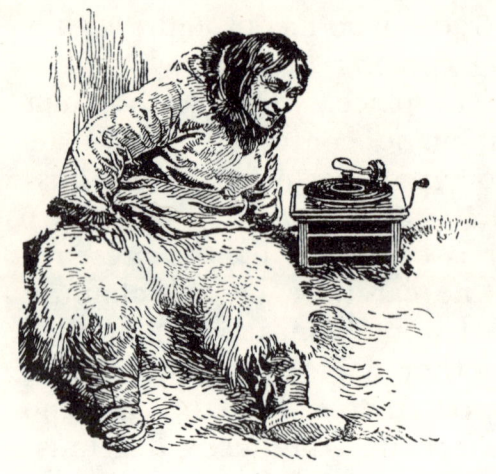

LISTENING TO A
HARRY LAUDER RECORD

Every trading post in the North has a number of Eskimo families attached to it who serve the post trader in various ways. These families usually build their igloos or set up their summer tents a short distance from the post, and as they are not wholly dependent upon hunting and fishing for their food they are not so migratory as less fortunate members of their tribes. In exchange for skins they get from the post trader many of the comforts of a white man's life and even some of the luxuries. If an Eskimo is lucky he buys a phonograph. As a race they have an excellent sense of rhythm and love stirring marches and gay songs. They are particularly fond of Harry Lauder records which make them laugh immoderately. The Eskimo laughs when he hears other people laugh whether he understands the joke or not.

As the spring sun mounts higher in the sky the

igloo walls begin to drip and the family prepares to forsake the winter home which has served them so well. They load up the omiak, the large skin canoe which they use for traveling and set off for the salmon fishing. A little later they will hunt "Mimeek," the eggs of wild fowl which are very numerous in early summer. They also go after wild berries—huckleberries and cranberries—which make an agreeable change in their restricted diet. Eskimos enjoy their short summer thoroughly and are always sorry when winter comes and drives them back to the igloo again.

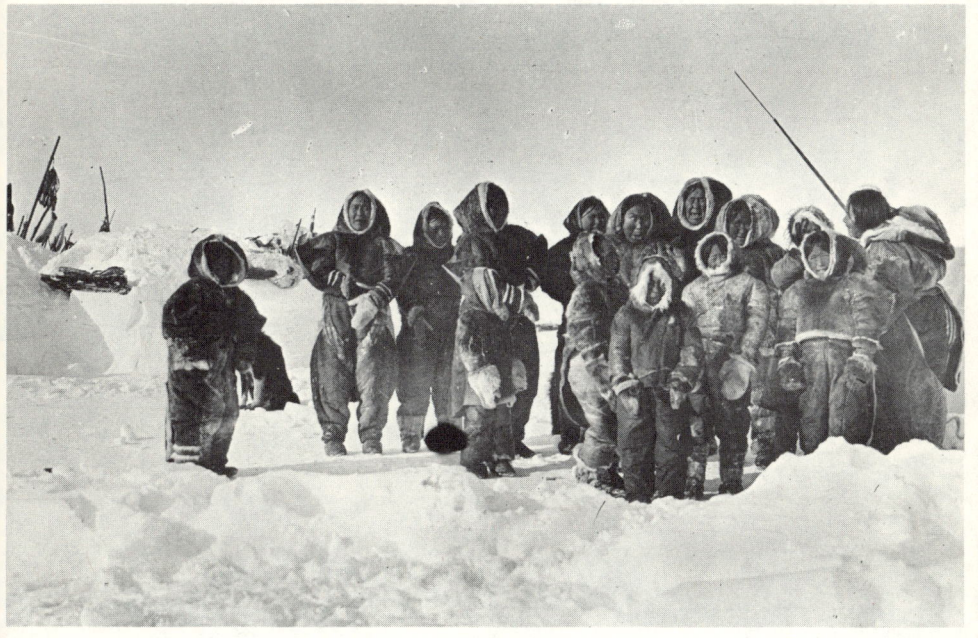

ESKIMO LIFE

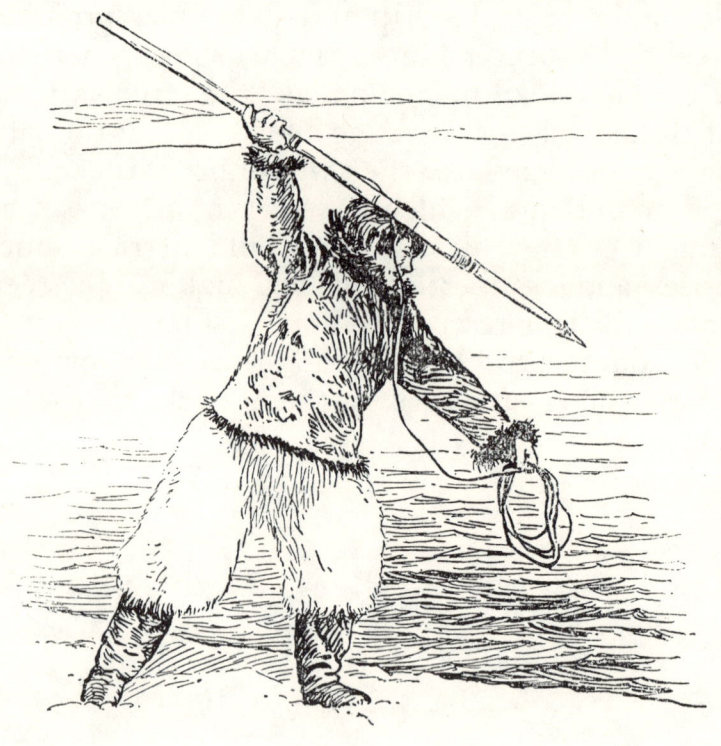

ESKIMO HUNTER
THROWING THE HEAVY WALRUS SPEAR

ESKIMO LIFE

A LIVELIHOOD IN THE ARCTIC

Famine is never far off in the North. Hunting and fishing are notoriously uncertain and hunger is a frequent and tragic visitor to the small Eskimo tribes. They have made little progress in the art of preserving food from time of plenty to time of scarcity, and make no provision for the future. The climate, of course, enables them to keep food in winter.

The sea provides walrus and seal, the land gives bear, caribou and many smaller animals. The great good luck of an Eskimo hunter is to spear a walrus. He makes the attack from a kyak or from the edge of an ice floe. A good hunter can send the spear fully forty feet and with momentum enough to kill a walrus weighing 2,000 pounds. He cannot haul this huge carcass ashore but he anchors it as best he can with the line of his spear until he can summon help. His friends and neighbors come eagerly to his assistance, for fresh, warm walrus meat is a great delicacy. The white man never quite gets over his repulsion to the way his Eskimo friends treat freshly killed game. They tear it to pieces and consume it at once without cookery or ceremony. A walrus will

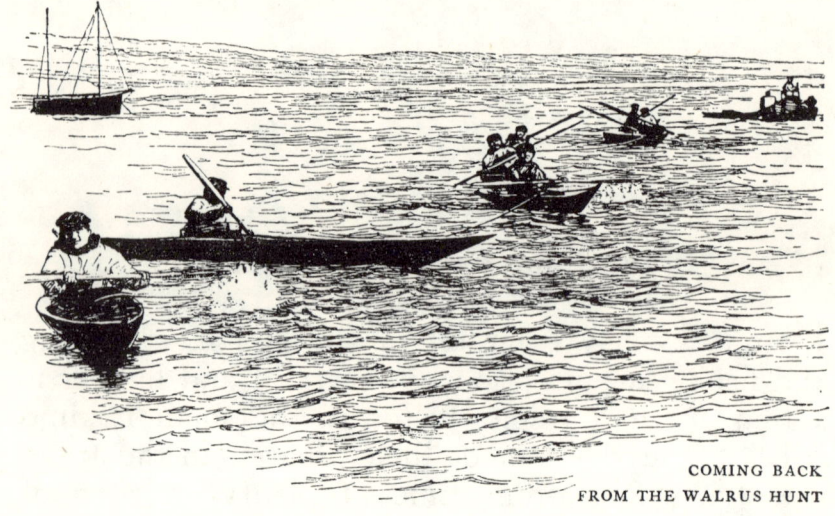

COMING BACK FROM THE WALRUS HUNT

provide not only a large quantity of excellent food but the hide makes a heavy, strong leather very useful for dog harness, whips, buckets and other utensils, while the tusks are valuable for spear heads or sledge runners. Eskimos usually hunt walrus in a fleet of kyaks, sharing the game if they are lucky enough to find it. Eskimos, like other primitive peoples are natural conservationists. They know nothing of sport in the white man's sense, and kill game only for meat or for the pelt.

The mainstay of a winter hunting season is the seal. As a seal is a mammal it must breathe about once in twenty minutes through a blow-hole in the ice. The hunter waits patiently over the hole with poised spear for the seal to come to the surface, but he is often disappointed as the seal is highly intelligent and provides a number of breathing places. When food is scarce an Eskimo will wait for hours, even days, at a seal hole. Should the weather be very severe he builds a wind break of snow blocks, in the same way as he builds the wall of his igloo, and spreads down a deerskin to stand upon while he waits. When the seal finally rises a quick, sharp thrust of the spear ends the long siege and there is seal meat for supper, seal oil for the igloo lamp and sealskin for the pliable, beautifully-made boots worn by every member of the Eskimo family except the baby.

These are not the fur seals used for coats, but various species of hair seals found near Hudson Bay. There is the common small seal found in all Canadian waters, the Harp seal and the Hood seal. The great prize is the Square Flipper seal, a huge creature weighing about 800 pounds and yielding a quantity of food and very superior leather. The illustration shows a small seal pup born in a blizzard which has matted his coat with frosty particles but

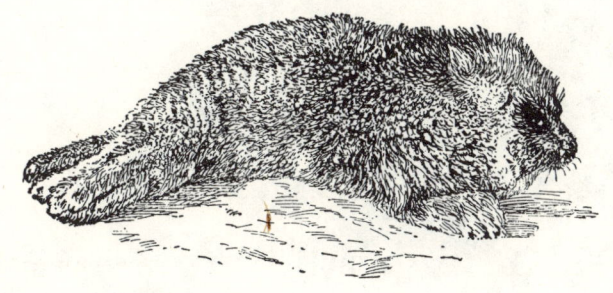

SEAL PUP
COATED WITH ICE

will not harm him in any other way. For about six weeks he will stay on the ice, after which he will crawl to the nearest creek and take his first swim under the instruction of his mother. At the same time he will learn to pick up his own living from the fish and shell fish which abound near land. This unusual photograph was taken near a Revillon Post in Hudson Bay.

The winter caribou is hunted for venison, which isn't particularly suitable for an Arctic diet as it is very deficient in fat, but chiefly for the skins which are warm and soft and make excellent winter clothing. Caribou skins are used with the fur either inside or outside, for trousers and for the hooded parkas. The large caribou hoods are usually edged with some longer fur like bear or fox. This is not a

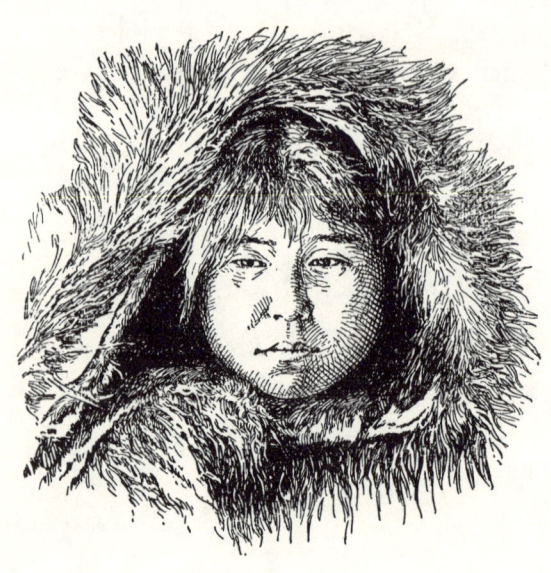

HOOD WITH BEARSKIN
BORDER TO PROTECT
THE FACE

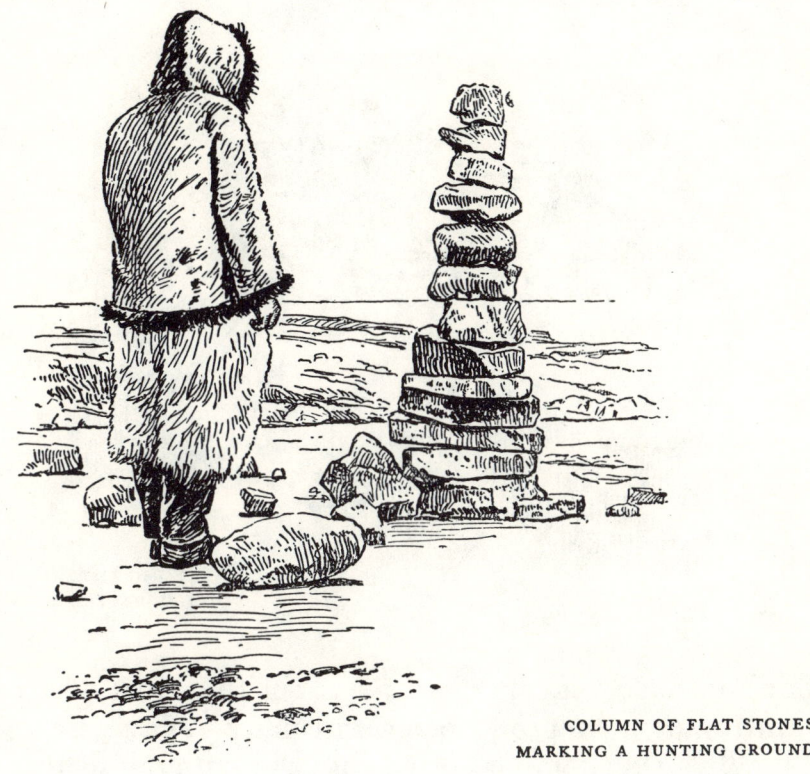

COLUMN OF FLAT STONES
MARKING A HUNTING GROUND

trimming put on for effect, though this combination of long and short fur is a favorite with fashion designers. The Eskimo uses it to keep the sharp sleet and snow from the face of the wearer and exclude the wind from the inside of the hood.

The northern landscape is always monotonous but especially so in winter when the drifting snows make it impossible to recognize even fairly familiar locations, so the Eskimo hunter builds landmarks of

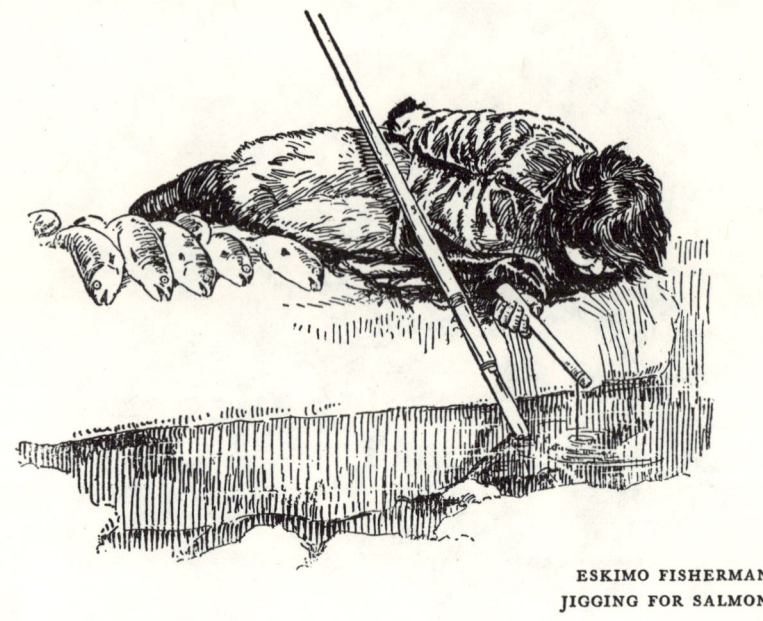

ESKIMO FISHERMAN
JIGGING FOR SALMON

flat stones so that he can find again the spots where hunting or fishing had been unusually good.

With the coming of spring the salmon fishing provides abundant food, excellent sport and an outing for the Eskimo family. The Eskimo makes a new salmon spear which is a tripod of two prongs of ivory and one of steel lashed firmly to a staff. A seal thong six or seven feet in length is attached to retrieve the spear after it is thrown. The Eskimo uses no bait in fishing but attracts fish with two ivory jiggers which he manipulates skilfully in a rift in the ice. When the fish rushes to this lure it is killed with the spear. The fisherman builds himself a sort of nest of twigs, driftwood or anything he can find to protect him from the ice on which he lies. Often the salmon fishing comes just in time to save whole tribes from succumbing to starvation.

The illustration shows the calendar of Kroonook, an Eskimo hunter who kept this interesting record of his year's work. The border around the edge represents the days, straight strokes for week days, crosses for Sundays. The pictures show deer of various sorts, a polar bear, walrus, readily distinguished by the tusks, and several varieties of seal and fish.

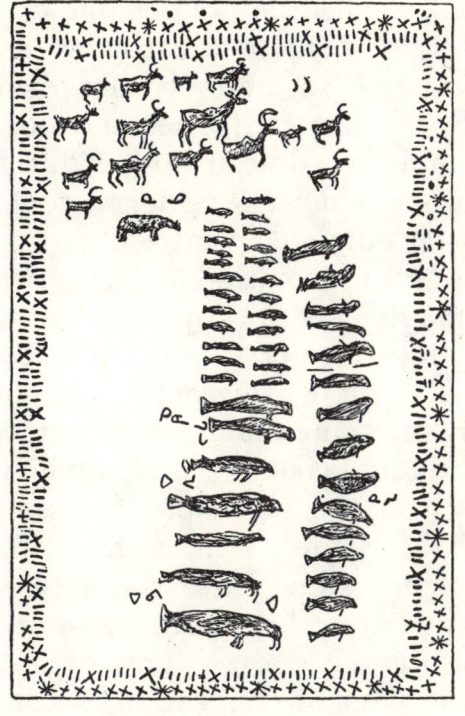

KROONOOK'S DIARY

THE EFFICIENT ESKIMO WOMAN

The Eskimo woman is indispensable to the economic life of the family. She does not hunt or fish if her husband is alive and well, but she skins with great skill the fur-bearing animals he captures, drying the pelts on home-made frames and dressing them to exquisite softness by her own primitive methods. She is hatter, furrier and boot maker to the entire family in addition to her duties as housewife and mother, which she performs conscientiously.

It must be admitted that she is an indifferent cook. It would be remarkable if she were anything else. Her family has no objection to raw meat or raw fish if they can get it when warm and freshly killed. This naturally discourages culinary effort. Until the trader came her utensils were very inconvenient. She could cook after a fashion in her heavy stone pots or in the water-proof vessels of walrus hide which she made for herself. By dropping a succession of hot stones into the stew it could be cooked in time but the result was not appetizing. Women who live near a post now have the enamelware pots and pans of civilization, and have learned something of the white man's cookery. They thaw

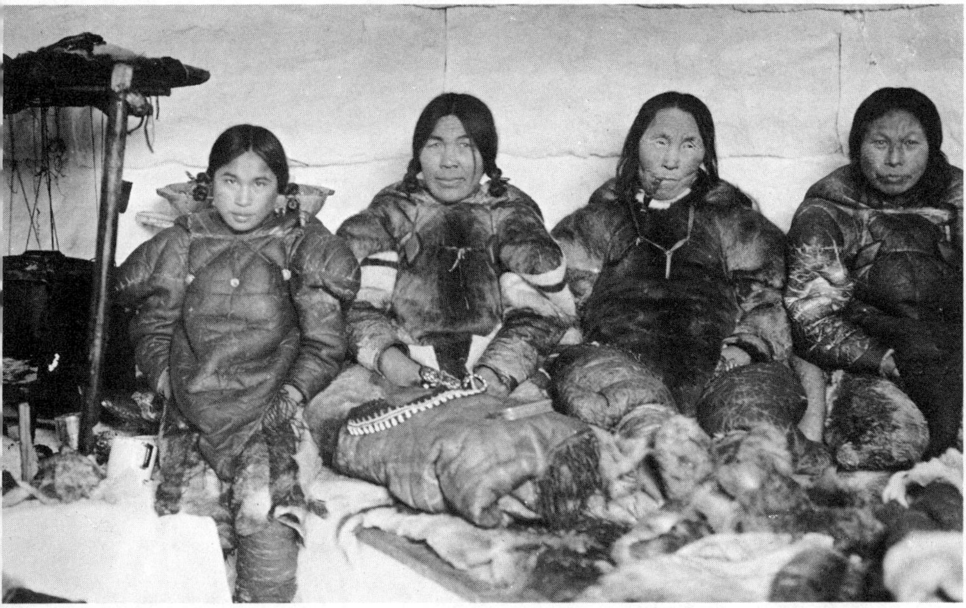

INTERIOR OF IGLOO

ESKIMO WOMEN AND CHILDREN

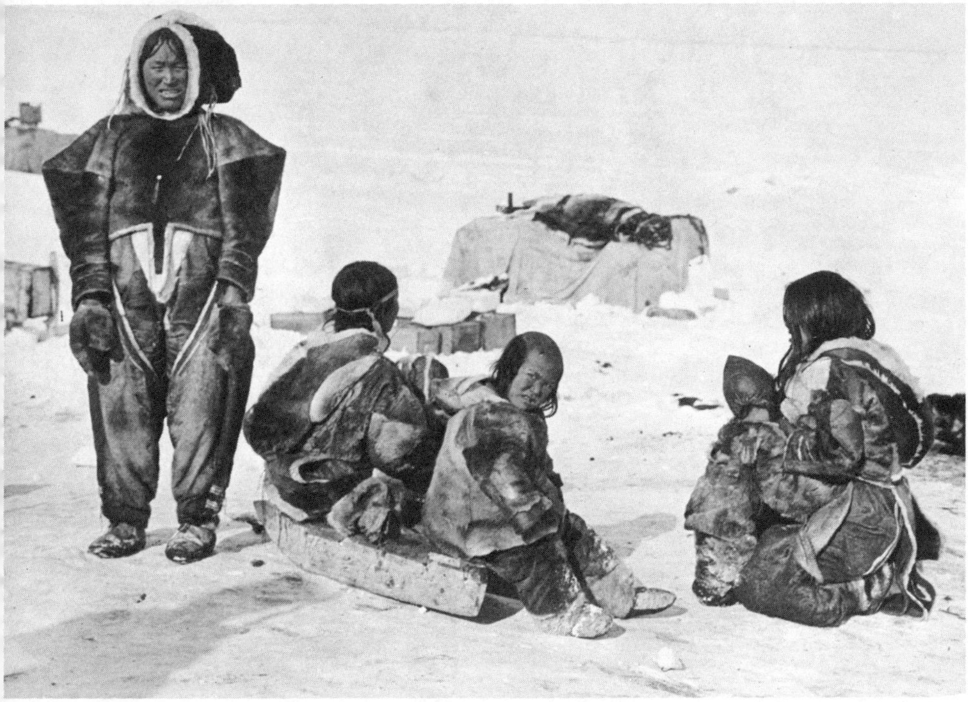

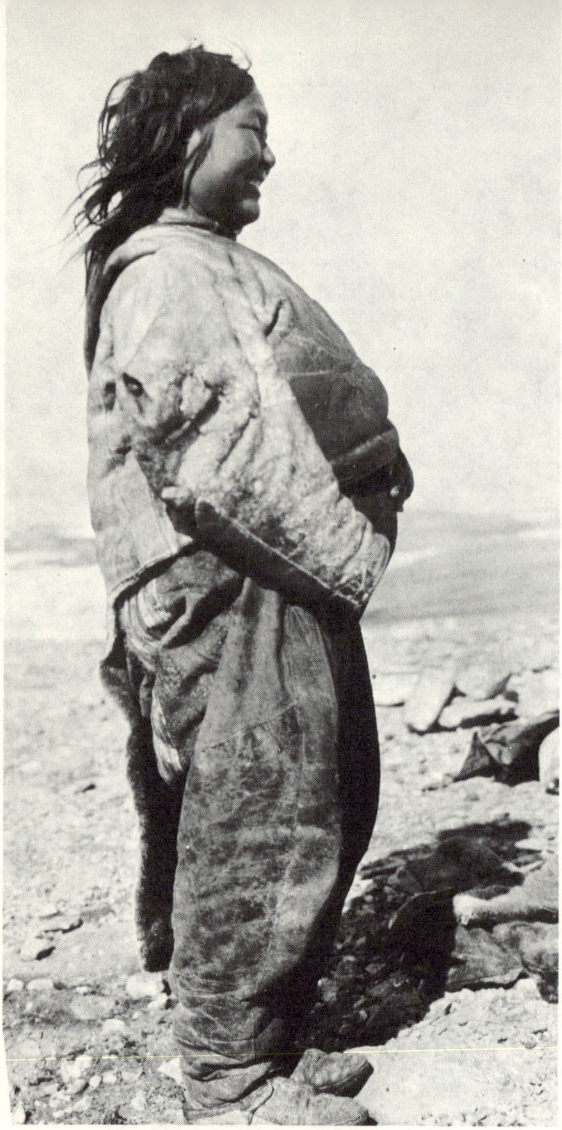

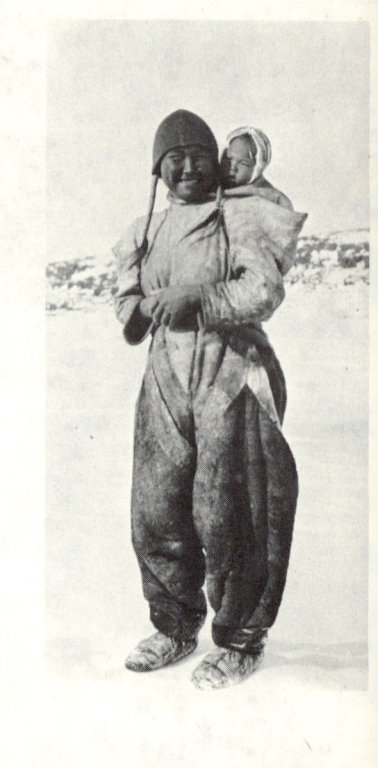

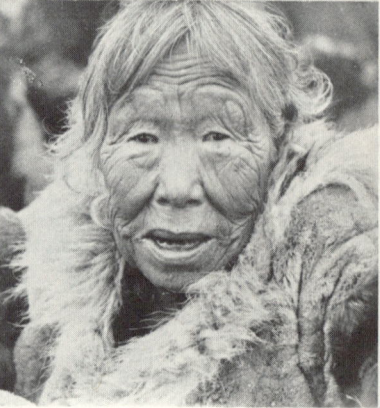

THE YOUNG AND OLD

ESKIMO LIFE

out their frozen meat and fish and have learned to use flour and beans and bacon, but in this land of frequent hunger any food is considered good and the preparation of it is of minor importance.

In making the family clothing the Eskimo woman shows great skill and a well developed decorative instinct. Her garments are well shaped and beautifully sewn and have that carefully studied fitness for their use which is characteristic of good clothes in Fifth Avenue or beyond the Arctic Circle.

The illustration shows a summer coat made from a blanket bought at the trading post. The large objects down the front which look like gigantic but-

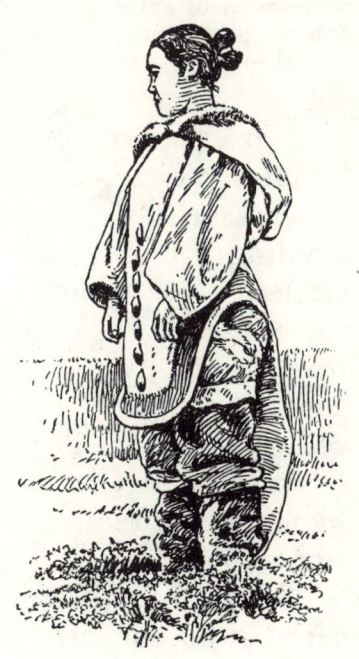

BLANKET COAT TRIMMED
WITH PEWTER SPOONS

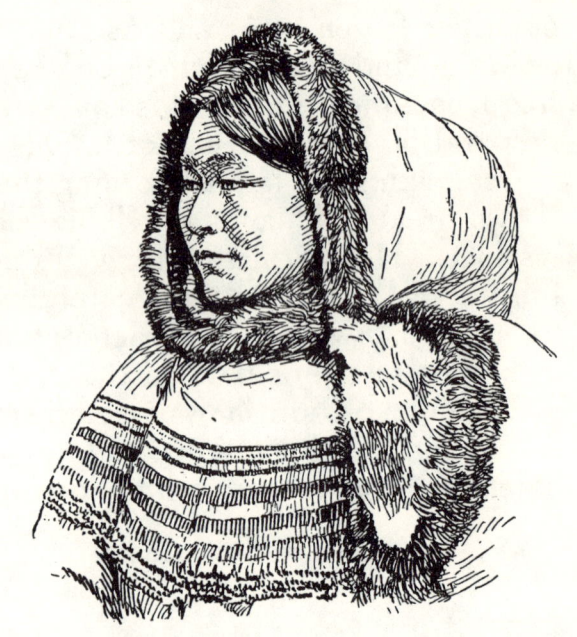

DEEP COLLAR OF BEADS
AND CARIBOU TEETH
IN DECORATIVE DESIGN

tons are the bowls of pewter spoons from which the handles have been removed. These rap on each other as the wearer stoops or sits with a pleasant tinkling sound which is excellent style in Eskimo circles. The women of the North like pretty things to wear as well as those of friendlier climates, and they cheerfully spend many hours of labor in making some articles of personal adornment. The large collar of beads illustrated above shows something of Eskimo ability in designing. The colors are handled as effectively as by some master of decoration.

The Eskimo woman's masterpiece is the shapely sealskin boots which she makes for the entire family.

They are warm, flexible and water-proof, securely sewn with the water-tight lockstitch which Eskimo needlewomen make so well. These boots are an ideal foot covering for a land of snow and ice and are very durable when the hard wear which they receive is considered. If a thaw comes the boots get wet and harden like all leather under similar conditions. They are then thoroughly dried on the racks outside the igloo or tent, or if the family is *en tour* on poles set up on the sledge or the omiak. Their maker then re-dresses them by chewing the leather until it is flexible.

One of the duties of the Eskimo wife is to make and attach the kyak cover of walrus skin or sealskin. This is the highest test of her craftsmanship as the

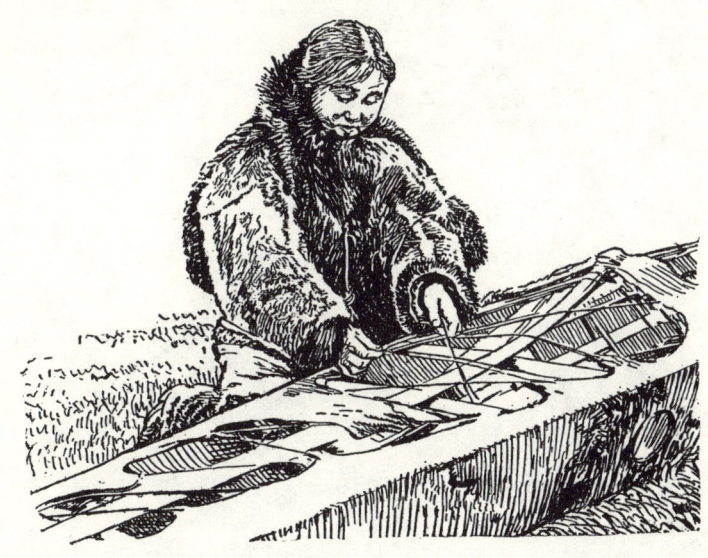

ATTACHING THE COVER OF THE KYAK

life of her hunter may depend on the quality of her work. The skins are sewed together with the lock-stitch and then laced on firmly as shown in the illustration. When put into the water they shrink and become taut like the head of a drum.

The Eskimo woman has a voice in the family councils and if the head of the family is needed for an expedition or to perform any unusual service for a white employer, the consent of the wife should first be secured. A diplomatic negotiator will do this with gifts of trinkets or useful articles for the home.

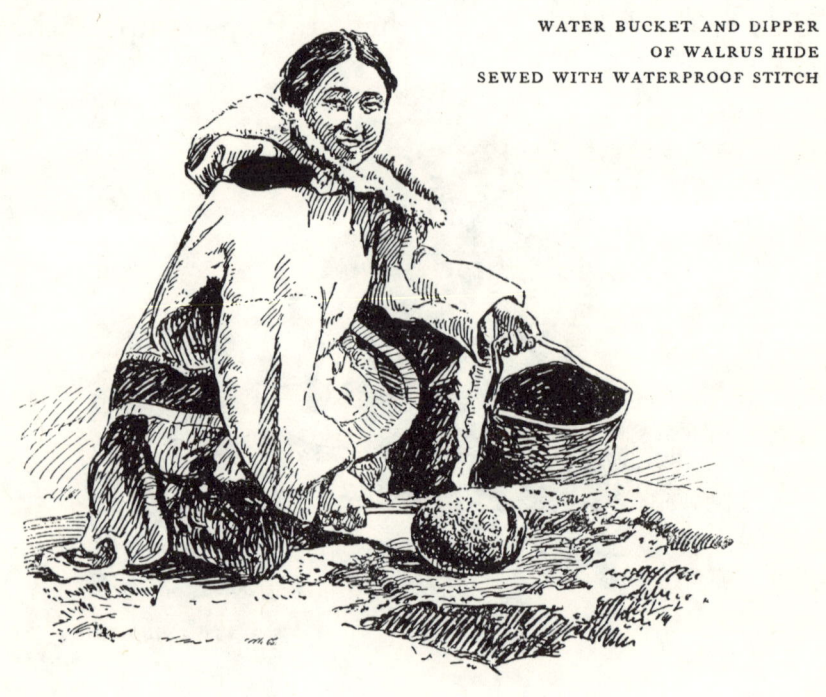

WATER BUCKET AND DIPPER
OF WALRUS HIDE
SEWED WITH WATERPROOF STITCH

FRIEND AND SERVANT—THE HUSKY DOG

The first playmate of an Eskimo child is the little Husky puppy, and as long as he lives the Malamute dog will be at the door of his igloo or his tent sharing his plenty or his poverty as the case may be. An Eskimo family is never without dogs unless the entire team has been swept away by one of the dreaded epidemics which attack them from time to time. When this happens the Eskimo starts to replace his loss as soon as he can possibly afford it.

Eskimo dogs are valuable, a good puppy bringing as much in this meagre land as a similarly well-bred young dog will cost at a metropolitan dog show. A good sledge dog costs from $60 to $100 which brings the price of a matched team to a very considerable figure. In the North, as elsewhere, certain individuals and certain trading posts have better luck in breeding dogs than others, so constant exchange is going on. An Eskimo will trade a fine rifle or a valuable bundle of skins for a dog he fancies, and the schooners which ply from post to post around Hudson and James's Bay usually have a dog pen filled with canine travellers on their way to a new home.

A sledge dog loves his work and is always eager

ESKIMO LIFE

to be off. The team howls and snarls as they draw their heavy loads, but if in good condition they are unwilling to rest until it is actually necessary. Eskimo drivers are usually kind to their dogs and rarely beat a tired animal though fighting or laziness is severely punished. When the dreaded soft snow comes in the North a driver will sometimes walk ahead of his team breaking a trail so that they can draw their load more easily. At the end of a hard day the face of a sledge dog will be covered with a mask of ice formed by his freezing breath.

Every dog team has its leader, a wise old fellow who pulls at the end of his trace, thirty feet or longer, and keeps the rest of the team in order with a rough and ready discipline. He must be the physical master of the team able to enforce his authority in

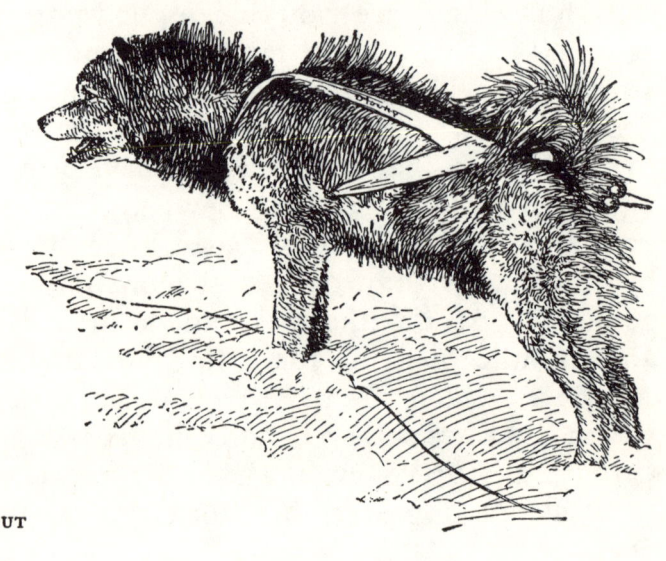

KEEPING
THE TRACES TAUT

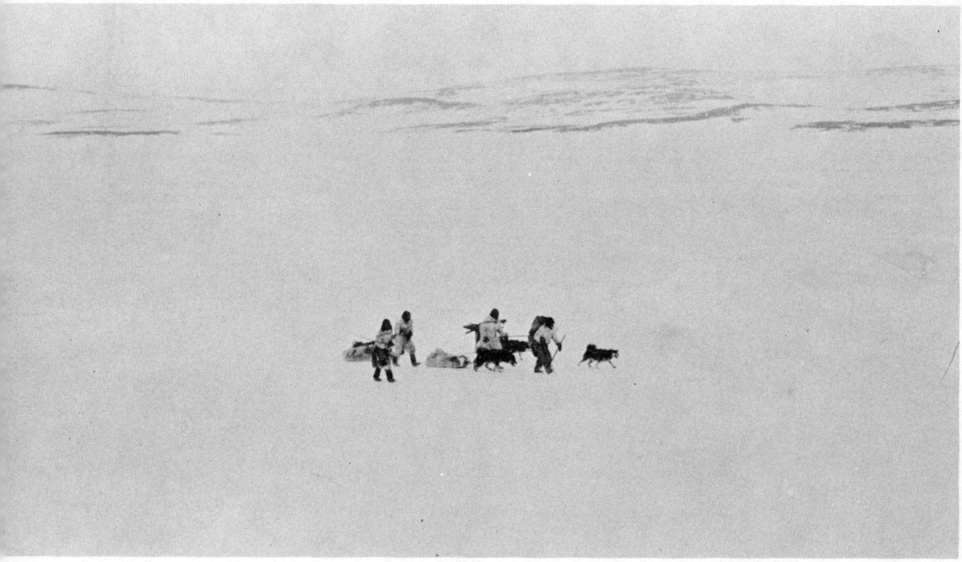

USING BEAR HIDES AS SLEDS ON SPRING ICE

DOG TEAM AND SLED AT EDGE OF ICE PACK

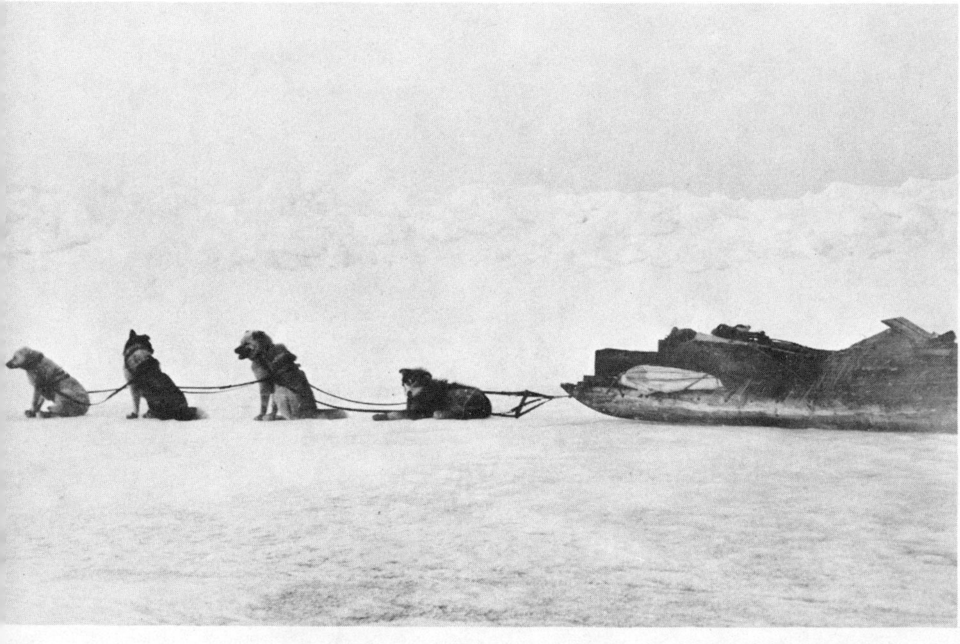

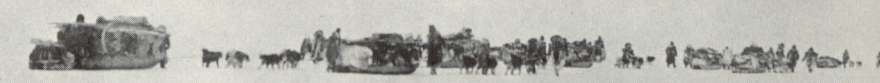

MOVING CAMP. TOTAL WORLDLY POSSESSIONS ARE TRANSPORTED BY SLED FROM ONE TEMPORARY HOME TO ANOTHER.

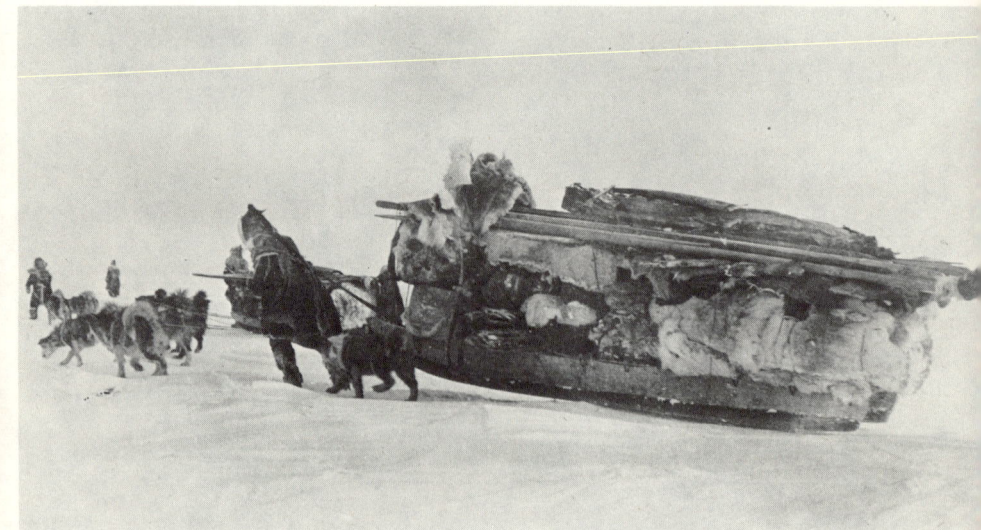

the quick, sharp fights which occur constantly. A well-bred sledge dog will respond to his driver's call which sounds like "Hu'it, hu'it" until he is exhausted. At the resting signal he will throw himself on the snow and relax completely until the word comes to go on.

At the post kennel the breaking in of a sledge dog begins when he is about half grown, but the Eskimo boys start much earlier, harnessing tiny puppies to their toy sleds and teaching them to pull the light burden. The puppy resists vigorously but soon learns that this is his destined task, and by the time he is strong enough to take his place in the dog team he knows his work pretty well.

An Eskimo dog will eat anything, including his own harness if his master is so careless as to leave it within reach. Omnivorous dog teams account for

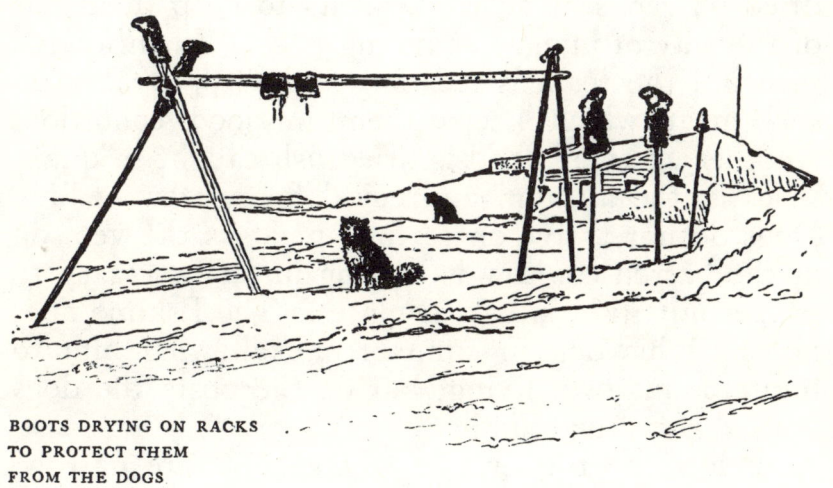

BOOTS DRYING ON RACKS
TO PROTECT THEM
FROM THE DOGS

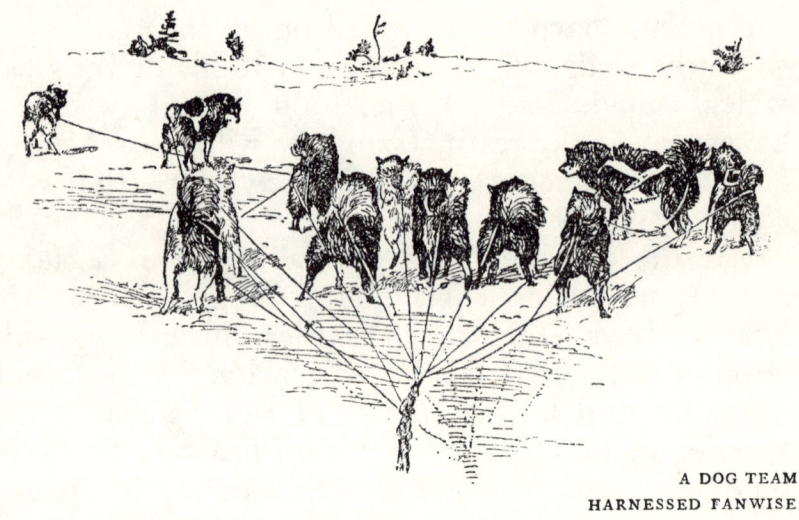

A DOG TEAM
HARNESSED FANWISE

many familiar sights in the North. In winter the kyak is stored on a high pedestal of ice or the dogs would eat the leather cover. Boots and clothing are dried on racks of poles or spears to keep them out of the way of hungry snapping jaws. When food is plentiful the team is fed once a day, preferably on seal meat which keeps them in good condition. Another excellent food is dried fish caught in quantities in the autumn and cured for winter feeding. Dogs do not thrive on caribou meat as the venison of the barren country is lacking in fat necessary to proper nutrition in cold climates. The Eskimo does not feed his dog in summertime allowing him to hunt for his own living, but at the posts the dogs are fed the year round.

Below the timber line where trails are narrow,

sledge dogs are harnessed in single file, usually four to the team. In the trackless open spaces further North the dogs are harnessed fan-wise which gives more power and better control to the driver but it necessitates stopping every few hours to untangle the traces which have become snarled through interweaving of the dogs. The leader dog on the longest trace is often a long way from the driver.

A dog sledge must be packed for safety in any position possible as it is sure to be turned over at least once a day and probably once every few hours. The guides are very skilful in preparing freight for a trip over the ice and it is not often that anything packed by an experienced guide is damaged. If a load collides with a boulder or ice cake and the master trace is broken the dogs keep right on running for a mile or two in the open country. The Eskimo driver does not pursue them, which he knows would be useless, but lures them back by craft. One method which is sometimes successful is to lie flat on the ice and imitate with the arms the flipper movements of a seal. The dogs come running back to investigate and are caught and re-harnessed.

Heavy snow which makes transportation so difficult in a country of railways and highways is eagerly welcomed in the North where the dog sledge is the only means of winter transportation. Distances which would be impossible on foot are readily covered with the dog team and the sledge on the hard-crusted snow or ice.

ESKIMO LIFE

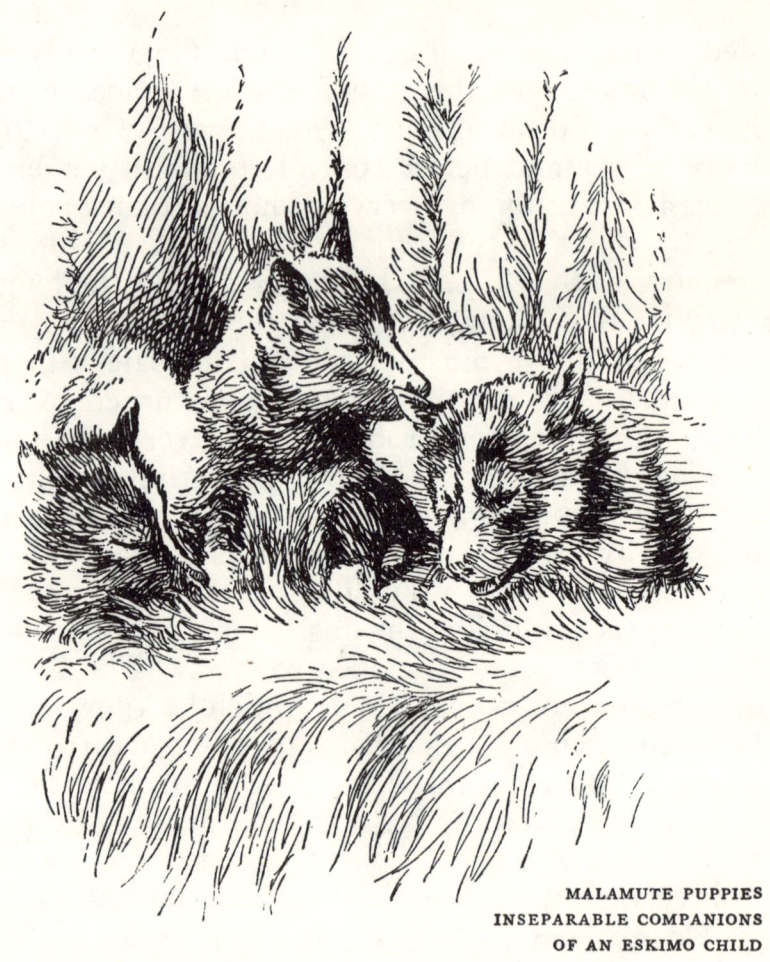

MALAMUTE PUPPIES
INSEPARABLE COMPANIONS
OF AN ESKIMO CHILD

ESKIMO LIFE

HAPPY LITTLE ESKIMOS

An Eskimo mother makes no baby clothes. The nude child lives in the great fur hood of the mother's deerskin coat in direct contact with her body until he is able to run about. Eskimo children are very beautiful. They are exquisitely formed and have a doll-like regularity of feature strongly Mongolian in type. Their hands and feet are small and shapely like those of the Japanese, and the Eskimo woman retains these shapely hands throughout life though she subjects them to the hardest labor.

Eskimo babies are nursed for two or three years as the food of adult Eskimos is highly unsuitable for infants. This long nursing period is one of the reasons why Eskimo families are never large.

Parents are tender and affectionate and Eskimo children are never spanked or corrected harshly. The children in turn are very obedient and loving and speak the words "Atata" (father) and "Anana" (mother) almost with reverence. They are very friendly to strangers. Instead of running away like young Indian children they approach a stranger confidently and smilingly. Having never experienced cruelty or rebuff they are unable to imagine it.

ESKIMO LIFE

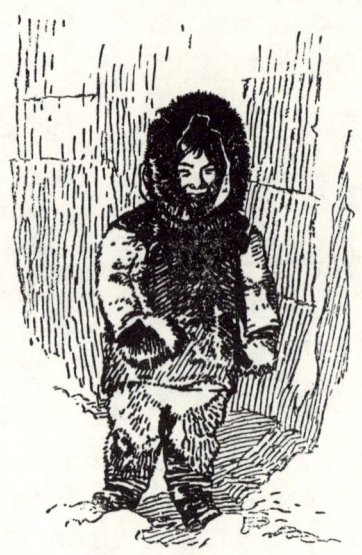

THE SENSIBLE DRESS OF AN ESKIMO CHILD

As they get older they perform small services for the white man with intelligence and faithfulness. The complicated camera which took the pictures from which these illustrations are drawn, was for many months in charge of a little Eskimo boy who protected it from injury with the greatest care.

As soon as a little Eskimo can run about freely he is clothed in an exact miniature of his father's costume, from the large loose hood on his caribou skin coat to the little warm water-proof sealskin boots just like those made for grown-ups. In these comfortable and well ventilated clothes he can play in the snow as much as he likes without danger of getting cold.

The first toy of a little Eskimo is his tiny sled just like the old-fashioned wooden sleds of American boys. For nine months in the year there is good sledding anywhere in the Arctic and Eskimo children play in the snow as other children play in sand or dirt. The first game naturally is harnessing the toddling puppies to the sled for a "mush" or journey over the ice around the igloo. Thus the child and dogs begin their lifelong companionship and dependance upon each other.

At the earliest possible moment an Eskimo father begins teaching his little son to use a bow and arrow. Sometimes he moulds little snow animals, bears and foxes, for the boy to aim at, and if the arrow shatters the toy the child and father are both well pleased. The use of the bow and arrow is not dying out in the North. For many purposes they are more practical

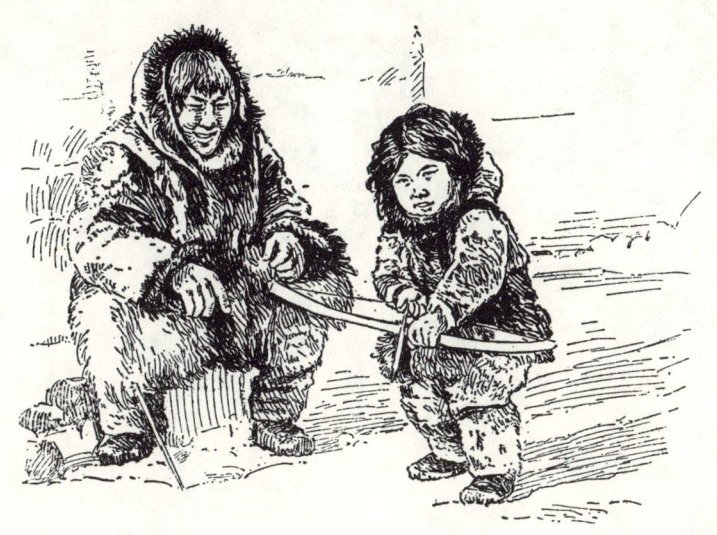

A LESSON IN MARKSMANSHIP

than the trader's guns and ammunition and learning to use the bow is an essential part of a young hunter's education. Revillon traders know instances where boys of eleven have caught several white foxes during the winter. At fifteen or sixteen an Eskimo boy is a good hunter and will go off by himself to get game.

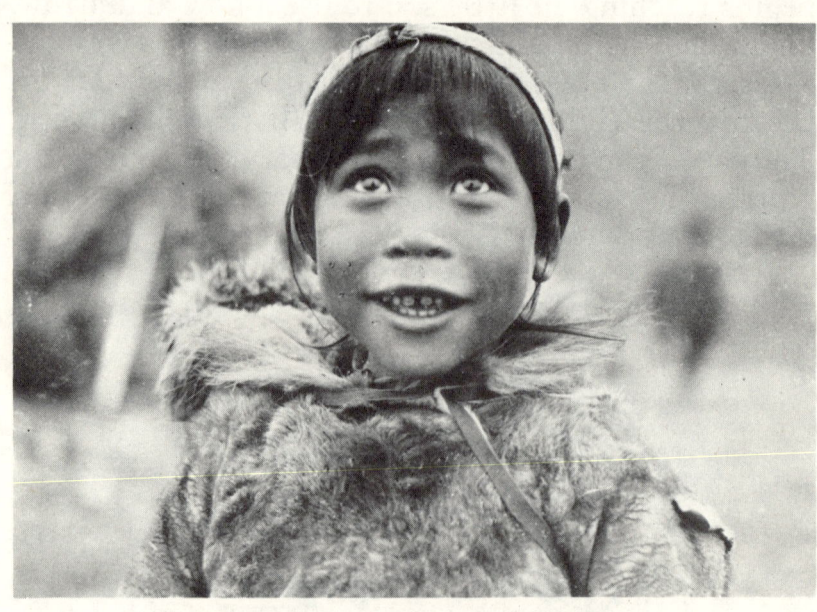

KYAK AND OMIAK

The Eskimo has two types of boat, the kyak, which the man uses for hunting and journeys and the omiak, a large canoe which will carry a dozen or more people with all their belongings. The omiak is for old people, women and children and is used mostly for spring migrations to new hunting and fishing grounds.

The kyak is a remarkable boat in both structure and performance. It is cranky and unstable to the last degree and the Eskimo owner handles it cautiously, but in skilled hands it will stand heavy seas and it is very speedy. A single Eskimo in a kyak will make better time than a crew of four in a canoe. He can keep up with a motor launch for a distance of several thousand feet and can perform amazing stunts in the handling of his craft. For voyages in heavy seas two kyaks are sometimes lashed together like a catamaran, but if the ropes wear away and the boats part the paddlers are drowned. The Eskimo, though an excellent boatman, never learns to swim in the icy Arctic waters which are open for such a short portion of the year.

The frames of Eskimo boats are made of almost

ESKIMO LIFE

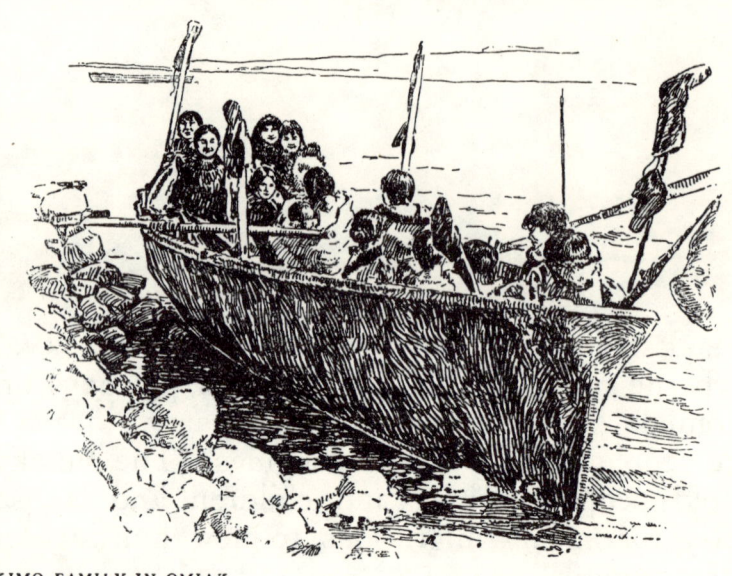

ESKIMO FAMILY IN OMIAK
NOTE THE SEALSKIN BOOTS
DRYING IN THE SUN

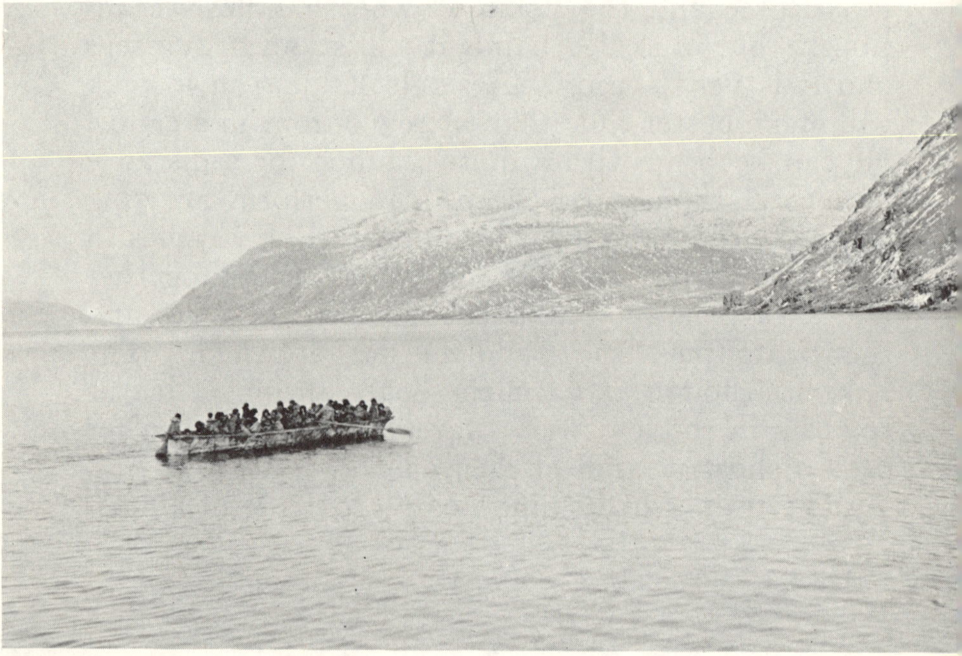

anything the builder can get. Driftwood is preferred but this is very scarce and is usually pieced out with bones and ribs of the larger animals. The sealskin cover joined by the Eskimo woman is laced securely over the hull and finished with a deck of skin leaving a circular opening for the paddler. This deck can be used for carrying fish or game or even a passenger who can remain sufficiently immovable to preserve the balance of the boat. Sometimes a passenger or freight is carried below decks, but the unstable character of the craft must always be taken into account. When traveling before the wind a small sail can be carried by a skilled boatman. Formerly these sails were made of grass matting or skins, but the Eskimo now buys a piece of canvas from the post trader.

When going hunting the Eskimo has his spear

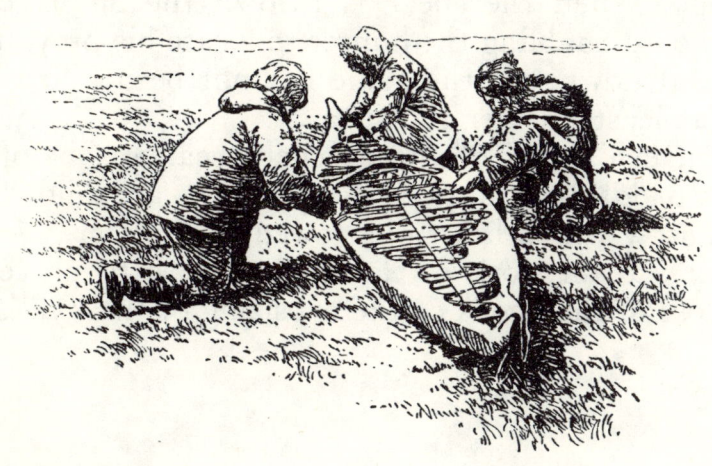

PREPARING THE KYAK
FOR LAUNCHING

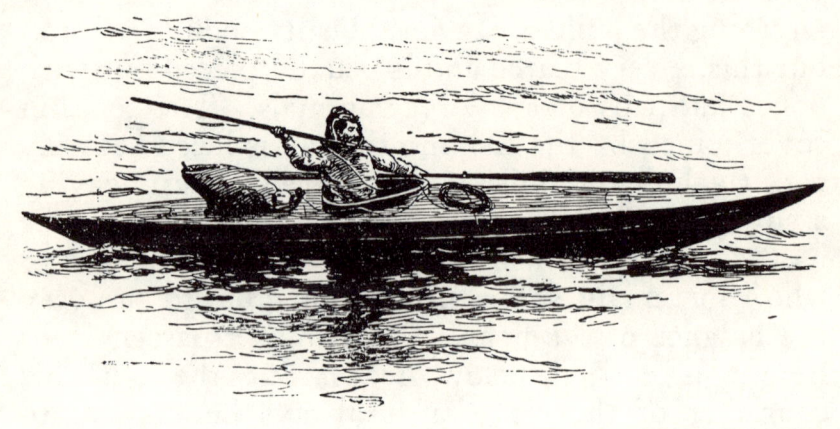

THROWING A SPEAR
FROM THE KYAK

lashed in a convenient position directly in front of him on the deck of the boat. On the after deck he carries a buoy made of inflated sealskin. This is attached to the head of the spear by a long seal-hide thong. When the spear is thrown the buoy goes overboard enabling the hunter to locate his prey and chase it down. If the game has not been killed he can at least recover the spear.

An exhibition of the excellent seamanship of a kyak paddler is afforded when supplies are unloaded on a scow which has to be towed to the pier. This requires team work of the highest type to prevent the loss of the goods or the capsizing of the kyak.

ESKIMO LIFE

FUR TRADING IN THE NORTH

The Arctic has only one industry—the taking of fur skins. The Eskimo hunter used to trap for his own food and clothing but he has now a market for his choicer peltry which enables him to get in exchange many things which add to his comfort and security such as firearms and ammunition for his own use, the poles and canvas for his summer home, thread and steel needles for his wife who used to sew with deer sinews and a bone needle, field glasses which enable him to see game a long way off, and the great steel snow knife which lasts so much better than his knife made of a walrus tusk though it does not cut the wet snow so well. The fur traders encourage the Eskimos to work more regularly for the sake of better food and the tools and implements which make his life easier.

Most important of all the post trader has brought to the North comparative freedom from famine which used to occur with tragic frequency. In the old days migration of game, a very severe winter, the loss of boats or dogs often meant starvation for large numbers of natives. When these disasters occur now the trading post has bacon, flour, beans and other necessaries and the Eskimo hunter's credit is good until the spring fishing comes or the game returns.

Revillon Frères maintain a chain of trading posts in the Eskimo country along the shores of James and Hudson Bay, where they collect marten, fox, bear and other skins of the region. Most of these posts are in touch with civilization only once a year when one of the Revillon schooner fleet brings in supplies and takes out the year's collection of peltry.

A trading post consists of five or six wooden buildings. As this country is practically barren the lumber must be brought from Montreal, a voyage of around three thousand miles. Buildings of a post are widely scattered to reduce danger from fire, and close by the main store and residence of the trader there will usually be a fire bell mounted in a tower. If fire breaks out this is sounded immediately to summon the employees of the post, including the Eskimos who are encamped nearby.

Eskimos bring in their skins on dog sledges, kyaks or in huge packs on their backs. The furs are wrapped in bales enclosed in a cover of deer skins strapped with raw moose hide. Skins shipped from the North have been well scraped and dried by the Eskimo and will keep indefinitely in this condition.

The Eskimos stay around the post for a considerable time selecting their supplies and enjoying a sociable holiday. They have many games interesting to the white man because they are so different from his own. One of them is a variation of tug-of-war. A stout circle of deer hide is slipped over the heads of the contestants and each man exerts his full strength to pull the other backward. An Eskimo boxing match is still more curious. The boxers pound away at each others' forearms with no attempt at parrying the blows and the man who can stand the pounding longest wins the match.

There are usually a considerable number of Eskimos encamped around a post in tents or igloos, according to the season. The post trader employs them for any work he may have under way and finds them intelligent and skilful at most of their tasks. At one of the posts there is a substantial stone pier which required several summers to build as every stone had to be carried and placed by hand. There are not, of course, even the simplest facilities for construction work in the North.

White men accustomed to the Arctic do not dread the long winters as they have borrowed from the Eskimo many of his devices which make the cold bearable. When the first snows come the trader has a shelter of snow blocks built entirely over the post, protecting it from the winds just as the igloo is protected. The entrance is through a snow tunnel built to the door in such a way that the wind cannot enter. The trading post becomes the center of its own little world locked away in the wilderness. The schooner has left coal, oil, food and other comforts. There is good fishing through the ice and usually excellent hunting if the trader has time for it.

Above all, there is interesting and responsible

work to be done. The trader must organize his own little world and make it as productive and prosperous as he can. He must be a good judge of furs and buy judiciously. The welfare of his dependents and the interests of his employees are always in his hands. A post trader must needs be a man of energy and resource and a real leader and executive. The freedom of the life attracts many such men of ability, and few who become established in the work ever leave it permanently. Once in three years a post trader has a furlough when he gets in touch with civilization and can make a fresh comparison of the advantages of life in the North and elsewhere.

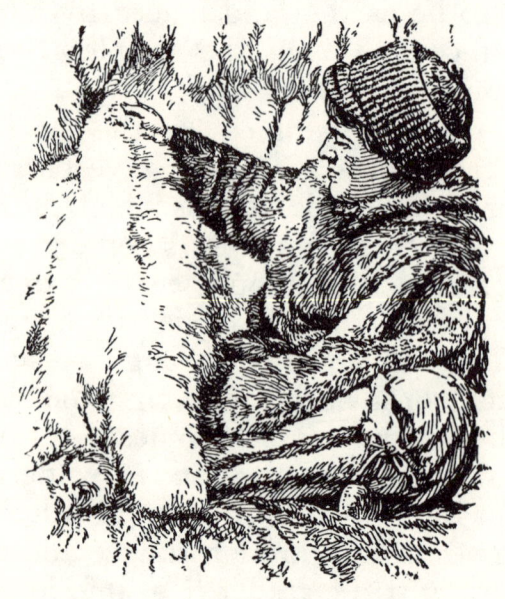

A POST TRADER
VALUING A SKIN